THE MERCY SEAT REVISITED STUDY GUIDE

by

Nigel Bovey

'Study to shew thyself approved unto God, a workman that needeth not to be ashamed, rightly dividing the word of truth' (2 Timothy 2:15 *King James Bible*).

UNITED KINGDOM TERRITORY
101 Newington Causeway, London SE1 6BN

To

Jo

(My mum, who taught me the value of study)

ISBN 978-0-85412-836-5

Major Nigel Bovey
was commissioned as a Salvation Army officer, with his wife
Margaret, in 1979. They have two children, Janine and Andrew.
Nigel previously taught Mathematics, Sociology and Economics
in a comprehensive school. He served as a corps officer in
Northern Ireland and England before being appointed to *The
War Cry* staff in 1994. As well as contributing chapters to a
number of books, he is the author of *Telling a Children's Story,
The Mercy Seat, Christians in the House, God, The Big Bang and
Bunsen-burning Issues* and *The Mercy Seat Revisited*. He is also a
published songwriter, lyricist and poet. He is the Editor of *The
War Cry*.

Scriptural quotations from the Holy Bible, New International
Version, copyright © 1973, 1978, 1984. Zondervan and Hodder
& Stoughton Limited.

Design consultant Stephen Pearson
Cover picture of the William Booth College mercy seat by Nigel Bovey

Printed by THQ Print and Design Unit

Contents

v

Registered users can download session worksheets from the
United Kingdom Territory infonet

Other readers may request session worksheets by emailing
publishing@salvationarmy.org.uk

Introduction

THE idea of this book is that it will help the reader delve deeper into some of the issues raised in *The Mercy Seat Revisited*. Officially it is a 'study guide', but I readily acknowledge that some people (myself included) find that label a bit off-putting. It smacks a little too much of flip-top school desks, black-stained inkwells and nostril-clogging chalk dust – and I was a teacher!

Since my first volume about the mercy seat was published in 1996, one phenomenon that has gained popularity – sadly, the two are not related – is the book club. Here, typically fortified by coffee and cake, a group of friends pick a book, read a chapter and then meet up to chat about what they've read. When they've finished that book, they choose another.

Before you choose another, may I say that this is how I see this book – as a conversation starter for friends. In that sense this book is a companion. I like that word. A compound deriving from the Latin *cum* ('with') and *panis* ('bread'), to companion literally means 'to bread with'.

My hope is that this book will be 'bread' to a reader's soul. It is not a substitute for *The Mercy Seat Revisited,* nor is it *The Mercy Seat Revisited Lite.* It is designed to be read with that book.

The topics and questions this companion raises are not the only ones that could be covered. You might rightly come to the conclusion that they are not even the best ones. That's why it is a conversation *starter*. The more friends talk to each other about the place and purpose of the mercy seat in The Salvation Army in general and in their corps in particular the better.

This book does not cover the issues raised in the appendices such as mercy-seat inscriptions and survey responses. It is expected that by the time twenty or so sessions have elapsed, a group will not need nudging into discussion. Appendix material can either be referred to when covering the relevant chapters or be used to kick-start further conversations.

Since *The Mercy Seat Revisited* was published in November 2010, I have been given more precious stories as to the benefits and value of the mercy seat. However you use this study guide – personally or in a group – I would be delighted to hear how your companioning is going.

My thanks, meanwhile, go to Major Leanne Ruthven, Editor-in-Chief and Publishing Secretary, for her encouraging oversight of this book, and to Major Philippa Smale, Literary Editor, for her characteristic care in rendering it fit for purpose.

Finally, I cannot but give thanks to God for another former schoolteacher, Maggie – my life's companion.

Nigel Bovey 2011

Chapter 1

Square One

IN Salvation Army worship the mercy seat is a special place that is used for a sacramental purpose. As such, those who go to the mercy seat, those who counsel them there and members of the witnessing congregation who engage in prayer support are all involved in a sensitive procedure.

In *The Sacraments: The Salvationist's Viewpoint*, it states: 'The Salvationist gives an honoured place in his meetings to the mercy seat.'

In *The Mercy Seat Revisited* the author makes the point that going to the mercy seat is 'the high point of Salvationist worship'.

The author observes that a sense of embarrassment or shame on the part of those moving forward from their seats to the front of the church appears to be absent in Anglican Communion services.

The author suggests that the language Salvationists use indicates how they view the mercy seat: 'The very words "penitent form" put the emphasis on the user or "seeker". If the person kneeling is a penitent natural curiosity demands to know: "What have they done that they're penitent about?"'

The author states: 'Every worshipper in every Salvation Army meeting should feel at total liberty and comfort to use the mercy seat as the Sprit leads.'

Head Space

1. In everyday life we increasingly see people leave flowers and candles at the site of roadside tragedies. Why is that, do you think?

2. What is your Square One? What do you see as the point and purpose of the mercy seat?

1

3. Why and when would you use the mercy seat? If you don't, why is that?

4. In your corps, how reluctant are people to use the mercy seat?

5. What barriers – physical, emotional and spiritual – are there to mercy-seat use? How can these be overcome?

6. In your corps, to what extent is the mercy seat regarded as a special place?

7. To what extent is there 'total liberty and comfort' to use the mercy seat during worship at your corps? How, if needed, could this be improved?

Heart Space

Pray for those who appear cold-hearted towards people making use of the mercy seat.

Pray that God will make you open-minded and open-hearted in your consideration of the mercy seat.

Ask God to give you the name of a person and pray for their salvation.

Chapter 2

They Shall Come From The East

THIS chapter starts to trace how and why the mercy seat became part of Salvation Army worship. Starting with the Cain and Abel offering (Genesis 4:3-4) in the opening pages, the sources of the current-day mercy seat rise in the biblical narrative and European evangelism before and after the Reformation and flow towards the New World of the 1600s.

The Salvation Army in the Body of Christ, a 2008 statement from the office of the General, states that mercy-seat use is one of the distinctives of Salvation Army worship: 'The Army has been led of God to adopt... its tradition of inviting people to respond to the presentation of the gospel message, and its use of the mercy seat for this and other spiritual purposes.'

The Old Testament records a basic human need to connect with the divine 'otherness'. The need to do something in response to God manifests itself in the complex system of offerings and sacrifices, as outlined by the Law, and by male circumcision.

In the New Testament, Jesus respects this longing to do something by calling people to follow him and adopt his lifestyle. For the Early Church, baptism becomes the outward action that witnesses to an inner transformation having taken place.

'Under Roman Catholicism,' writes Alan Streett in *The Effective Invitation*, 'sinners were saved by the church, not by the atoning death of Christ.' There were, however, preachers who believed that salvation comes through repentance and faith in Christ. They called people to do something in response to God.

Some Presbyterian churches used to use a cutty stool to discipline its members. Those who had broken church rules were required to sit or stand on the stool in full view of the congregation until they had repented.

Head Space

1. What aspects of Salvation Army worship make the Army distinctive?

2. Read Leviticus 1 to 7 and Hebrews 9. What strikes you about the difference between the giving of offerings and making of sacrifices in the two passages?

3. Think of, or discover, other New Testament verses which highlight the kind of sacrifice Christians should make. How would you describe the kind of response God asks from us?

4. How can you tell if someone is a Christian?

5. How helpful is it for the mercy seat to be used as a place of discipline – asking people who have fallen out or who were once soldiers and now want to be reinstated to go to the mercy seat during a meeting as a precondition of their reacceptance?

Heart Space

Pray for those people you know who have lost, or who are struggling in, their faith. Ask God to show you if you should reach out to those who used to worship at your corps but who no longer worship anywhere.

Offer to God your willingness to be a living sacrifice for him.

Chapter 3

They Shall Come From The West

IN the early 1600s various Protestant groups fled persecution in Europe, crossed the Atlantic in search of religious freedom and started to paint America's spiritual landscape. During the Great Awakening of the 1730s a quarter of the population was converted to Christ. One of the features of the subsequent emerging American church was the use of the altar call and the institution of a special place to which people should go in response.

During the Great Awakening, the standard method of asking people to respond after a sermon was for them to speak privately with the preacher after the service.

In Britain in the late 1700s, John Wesley invited people to respond by calling them to a bench or seat at the front of the church. This mourner's bench or anxious seat was a forerunner of the Army's penitent form or mercy seat.

In America, the camp meetings of the Second Great Awakening (1795-1835) were characterised by people being invited forward, sometimes to stand, sometimes to sit or kneel at a mourner's bench.

Presbyterian evangelist Charles Finney championed the use of the altar call, often but not exclusively calling people to an anxious seat.

Opposition to such soul-saving methods started almost as soon as they were first used. Among the early-day dangers noted were that mercy-seat use could be insincere and that the act of going forward might be interpreted as meaning that unless someone went forward they could not be saved.

Head Space
 1. Can somebody pray at the mercy seat for too long?

2. Where is the benefit in making a public response at the mercy seat as opposed to responding to God, or seeking spiritual counsel, privately?

3. What helpful alternatives to mercy-seat use are there?

4. To what extent do we need to make our response to God public?

5. What misconceptions are there about mercy-seat use?

Heart Space

Thank God for the courage and conviction of Christians who were and are prepared to try new things for the gospel.

Ask God if there's anything new you could be doing to extend his Kingdom.

Pray for those who will lead worship next week, that God will speak to them in preparation and through them in presentation.

●

Chapter 4

The Mercy Seat and William Booth

THE revivalist mourner's bench became the Army penitent form thanks largely to the influence of Methodist evangelist James Caughey. The Irish-American Caughey had seen the mourner's bench in use during the Second Great Awakening and adopted it into his ministry. In 1846, he preached in Nottingham. One of the young lads to respond to God that night was a certain William Booth. From an early age, Booth was convinced of the benefit of calling people to public decision.

Before he and Catherine founded The Salvation Army, William adopted the practice of calling people forward to a bench in response to God. This met with opposition from some of his Methodist colleagues. Nevertheless, convinced of Caughey's methods, Booth persisted.

Like her husband, Catherine was an ardent advocate of the mercy seat. In 1876, against representations that the Christian Mission should abolish the mercy seat, she addressed the annual conference: 'Whomsoever it may offend or please, I am going to have a penitent form.'

When an itinerant preacher, Booth sometimes invited seekers to kneel at the Communion rail of the host church.

Throughout Booth's ministry, critics argued that his calling of people to the mercy seat was emotionalism – that he was playing to their feelings.

Speaking about the mercy seat, Booth once declared: 'I delight in it. I am married to the penitent form.'

In his book *General Booth*, George Scott Railton writes of the Founder: 'He probably led more souls to the penitent form than any man who had ever lived.'

Head Space

1. What are today's objections to mercy-seat use?

2. What part, if any, should emotion play in inviting people to use the mercy seat?

3. How can those who get emotional at the mercy seat be most sensitively helped?

4. How did Booth lead so many people to find salvation at the mercy seat?

Heart Space

Thank God for the people who have had a godly influence on your life. Ask God to empower you, so that you in turn are a godly example to others. Invite God to touch your whole being afresh: body, mind and emotions.

Chapter 5

The Centre of Gravity

AN 1898 *War Cry* report of William Booth's farewell meeting in the Royal Albert Hall before leaving for the United States described the mercy seat like this: 'The penitent form which, so to speak, is the beautiful centre of gravitation round which all the Army's efforts arrange themselves.'

Over the years the mercy seat has become the centre of gravity of Salvationist identity. Millions of people have gravitated to the mercy seat and found salvation. Millions more have sensed a divine pull to the mercy seat and there discovered help, healing and holiness.

This chapter (together with Chapter 7) traces some of the major developments of the mercy seat, from being something about which the Booths were personally convinced to its becoming the universally acknowledged place of prayer within Salvationist worship.

In the first of many such subsequent reports, the launch issue of *The Salvationist* (1 January 1879) records: 'A cock fighter came to a meeting under the influence of drink, but he was very soon under the influence of the Spirit. He was convinced of sin, came to the penitent form, gave his heart to God, and is now rejoicing.'

The existence of the mercy seat came to the attention of the Skeleton Army, persecutors of early-day Salvationists in the UK.

Between 1881 and 1885, Robert Sandall records in *The History of The Salvation Army*, 250,000 people knelt at Army mercy seats.

The terms 'penitent form' and 'mercy seat' were in official use by the early 1900s.

In the trenches of the First World War, at least one Salvationist used his military greatcoat to make a mercy seat and invited his regimental pals to find peace with their Maker before they met him.

Over the years Salvationists have shown similar ingenuity in adapting and using objects other than a wooden bench as a mercy seat. These include penitent mats, prayer mats, sand sculptures, gym benches and bass drums.

Head Space

1. Why is current mercy-seat use in the UK not measured in the thousands?

2. To what extent does persecution affect people's readiness to respond to God?

3. What difference in emphasis, if any, is there between the terms 'penitent form' and 'mercy seat'?

Heart Space

Reflect on the fact that many early-day Salvationists faced physical danger and persecution for being Salvationists.

Pray for Salvationists and other Christians who today face persecution and peril for their faith.

Ask God to give you and your corps a longing to see people saved, the ideas to make the gospel relevant to those around you, the patience to listen to God and the power to do what he asks.

Chapter 6

The Mercy Seat and Brengle

IT may have been William Booth who brought the penitent form to the Army, but it was Samuel Logan Brengle who brought the Army to the penitent form. Arguably the greatest mercy-seat exponent and front-line fighter, Brengle saw the penitent form as the birthplace of The Salvation Army.

In *Love-Slaves* he writes: 'The Salvation Army was born, not in a cloister, nor in a drawing-room, but on a spiritual battlefield – at the penitent form.'

In *Samuel Logan Brengle: Portrait of a Prophet,* Clarence Hall recognises that 'the penitent form was the immediate goal, the focal spot, toward which Brengle's every point in his meeting technique turned'.

From January to June 1919, Brengle witnessed more than 3,000 people kneel at the mercy seat in meetings he conducted. Brengle's passion for the penitent form (he never referred to it in his writings as the 'mercy seat') was characterised by:

- Personal prayer: 'I have carried a penitent form around in my heart for half a century or more. And if there is ever any need, I constantly fly there.'

- Corporate prayer: 'I attended an all-night of prayer. It was a blessed time and scores of people sought the blessing of a clean heart.'

- Personal commitment: 'I seldom let anyone leave my penitent form without dealing with him myself.'

- Perseverance: 'There was only one unsaved person left in the hall... We turned our attention to her and soon she was on her knees in the middle of the hall, where she got saved.'

- Sensitivity: 'Permit me to suggest that, when people have reached the penitent form, they be allowed to kneel in silence before the Lord for a time without having two or three people come to question them and pour advice into their ears... We must not hurry people into the Kingdom at the penitent form.'

Head Space

To what extent are the above qualities evident in your own life and in the corporate life of your corps?

Heart Space

Reflect on the qualities that made Brengle's soul-saving work so effective. None of us is another Brengle, but we can give God everything we are – and gain from him the spiritual resources we need – to be people who attract others into his Kingdom. Offer yourself afresh to him. Receive afresh from him. Know that his Spirit is alive in you and is willing to flow through you to others.

Chapter 7

The Focal Point In Focus

THE *Salvation Army Year Book* describes the mercy seat as 'a focal point to remind all of God's reconciling and redeeming presence'. (For the full definition, please refer to Chapter 2, page 9 of *The Mercy Seat Revisited*.)

In 1996 the International Spiritual Life Commission convened to 'review the ways in which The Salvation Army cultivates and sustains the spiritual life of its people' – in other words, to refocus the movement on its spiritual resources and practices. It subsequently issued a number of calls to the global Salvation Army, including one to the mercy seat.

Part of the call reads: 'We affirm that the mercy seat in our meetings symbolises God's unremitting call to his people to meet with him. It is not only a place for repentance and forgiveness, but also a place for communion and commitment. Here we may experience a deep awareness of God's abundant grace and claim his boundless salvation. The mercy seat may be used by anyone, at any time, and particularly in Army meetings when, in response to the proclaimed word, all are invited to share loving and humble communion with the Lord.'

Over the years, Salvationist writers have pondered the philosophical aspects of the mercy seat. What does it mean? What is its purpose?

Wesley Harris writes that to have a Salvation Army without the mercy seat would be like having 'wheels without hubs'.

George Carpenter sees the mercy seat as a guest room, a place for prodigal home-coming.

For Alfred Cunningham the mercy seat is a labour ward: 'the place of the coming to birth of the new life.'

Linda Bond sees the mercy seat as 'one of the most basic and profound symbols of all that we are – a salvation people'.

Sarah-Jane Gregory, describing how children at her corps regard the mercy seat, writes that they liken it 'to the "friendship bench" in the school playground where someone sits when they are lonely and want someone to play with'.

As well as philosophical, there are practical implications. Some corps have a moveable mercy seat. UK legislation requires a mercy seat in a new or refurbished hall to offer easy access for people with disabilities. There are also health and safety considerations when using a public venue. Amid of all of this Salvationists are challenged to keep their focus on the place, purpose and potential of the mercy seat.

Head Space

1. How would you describe the mercy seat?

2. What should the mercy seat be used for?

3. How convenient is it to be able to use the mercy seat at any time during worship?

4. What do children teach us about using the mercy seat?

5. What barriers are there to using the mercy seat?

Heart Space

Thank God that around the world people are responding to God at the mercy seat.

Ask God to help you focus on the place, purpose and potential of the mercy seat in your own life and in the life of your corps.

Chapter 8

All Over The World

AS a distinctive of Salvation Army worship, the mercy seat is used in every part of the Army world. There are, however, regional variations. For example, in the United States, where it is generally referred to as 'the altar', it is the practice at some corps for people to pray, alone or as a family, at the mercy seat before the holiness meeting begins. By contrast, some corps in Australia invite people to receive prayer and counselling at the mercy seat after the conclusion of the meeting.

In some territories, the mercy seat is in frequent use; in others, people use the mercy seat only for landmark commitments.

Common global characteristics include:

• meeting leaders giving an invitation for people to use the mercy seat, although mercy-seat use is not dependent on such invitations

• the mercy seat being used as a place for people seeking salvation or sanctification

• the mercy seat being used as a place for covenant-making, intercession, petition, thanksgiving and dedication

• mercy-seat users being offered the option of prayer and spiritual counsel.

Head Space

1. How helpful do you find it that the mercy seat can be used for any response to God, and not just for coming to faith and being filled with the Holy Spirit?

2. What, if anything, should be done to broaden the appeal and use of the mercy seat in your corps?

3. To what extent can frequent use of the mercy seat be as problematic as little or no use?

4. How can the notion that the mercy seat is the place to go only to be saved or sanctified be best addressed?

Heart Space

Thank God for the fact that The Salvation Army is at work in more than 120 countries around the world.

Pray for Salvationists, by name if you know them, who serve the Lord in a country other than your own.

Ask God to broaden your horizons on the work, witness and worship of the international Salvation Army.

Chapter 9

The Holiness Table

WHILE information can be gathered about the place and purpose of the mercy seat, there is far less data about how, when and why the holiness table became part of Salvation Army furniture. The received wisdom is that early-day meeting leaders would invite people seeking salvation to kneel at the mercy seat and invite Christians seeking the power to live a holy life to the holiness table, which typically was situated in front of the mercy seat.

According to my 2009 territory-wide survey, holiness-table use in the UK is on the increase. However, it is not used solely – or even extensively – as the focal point for seeking sanctification. It is also used as a mercy-seat alternative for those who cannot kneel, an overflow when the mercy seat is full and a place to deposit the offering plates, commitment cards, altar-service envelopes and the weekly flowers.

Across the world, holiness-table use ranges from the original function – the place to go to receive the blessing of holiness – to being completely absent from the building. A number of territories do not have holiness tables in their halls.

The global overview is that – with a few notable exceptions, mainly in the United States – the holiness table is not being used as originally intended.

Head Space

1. If it has one, how does your corps use the holiness table?

2. What virtue is there in having a separate place where Christians may receive spiritual cleansing and resources?

3. How would your corps benefit were the holiness table to be reintroduced as a focal point for personal sanctification?

4. The Salvation Army has been characterised as being birthed in the holiness movement. To what extent are Salvationists losing sight of the importance, vibrancy and possibility of personal holiness?

Heart Space

Thank God for the possibility of knowing his forgiveness, restoration and cleansing in your life.

Confess those areas of your life, those attitudes and actions that need his cleansing.

Invite him to fill you with the graces and gifts of the Holy Spirit.

Commit yourself to putting his word into action in your life.

Chapter 10

Cue For A Song

ONE of the areas considered in *The Mercy Seat Revisited* is how Salvationists, past and present, perceive the mercy seat. What is its purpose? What truths does it represent? What does it achieve? What does using it signify?

Chapters 10 to 12 outline a collection of mercy-seat perceptions through song, poetry and personal reflection. Appendices A and D reflect the thinking of hundreds of present-day UK Salvationists about the mercy seat. Appendix B records the perceptions of former Salvationists who outlined the purpose of the mercy seat through 'mission-statement' inscriptions.

The Salvation Army Song Book, and before it *The Christian Mission Hymn Book*, has always contained a number of songs referring to the mercy seat.

Fifteen songs in the 1986 edition contain references to the mercy seat. Of the nine that were written by non-Salvationists, eight were written before the Army started.

In the 20th century, all new additions to Army song books on the subject of the mercy seat came from Salvationist writers. Once in Salvationist hands, it becomes less clear whether the mercy seat in a song refers to the physical bench in the Army hall, the figurative concept of communion, comfort and contrition it embraces, or both.

The fact that these songs are still included in the song book and are in current use suggests that Salvationists approve of the mercy-seat pictures painted by the songs.

Head Space

1. As you read through the lyrics, which words and phrases most closely reflect your perception of the mercy seat?

19

2. Which, if any, song book word-pictures connected with the mercy seat do you find unhelpful, and why?

3. From your experience, what areas, if any, do these songs leave uncovered?

Heart Space

·Thank God for the gift of songwriting.

Pray for songwriters, by name, asking that God will continue to inspire and ignite them.

Choose one of the songs from the chapter and make it your prayer for mercy-seat use in your corps.

Chapter 11

The Mercy Seat In Verse

THE mercy seat is the object of poetic focus. The poems collated in Chapter 11 are a selection, rather than a complete anthology, of mercy-seat inspired verse. Like the songs of Chapter 10, they are a mixture of perceptions and insights on the biblical mercy seat and the Salvation Army prayer bench.

Head Space

1. As you read the poems, which words and phrases reflect your perception of the mercy seat?

2. Which, if any, of the word-pictures connected with the mercy seat do you find unhelpful, and why?

3. Identify a line or verse that you find particularly moving.

4. From your experience, what areas, if any, do these songs leave uncovered?

Heart Space

Thank God for the gift of poetry.

Pray for poets you know, by name, asking that God will continue to inspire and ignite them.

Choose a couple of lines or a verse and make it your prayer for mercy-seat use in your corps.

Chapter 12

Personal Reflections

FOR most Salvationists the true value of the mercy seat is not found in prose or poetry but in personal use. The mercy seat is a special, sacred place where they make life-changing decisions and meet with their Lord. Years later they may not recall the exact wording of their prayer but they will remember the occasion.

The collection of personal reflections in Chapter 12 is in no sense systematic, statistical or scientific. They are not representative of age, race, status, gender or any other indicator so loved by pollsters and statisticians. They cannot be said to be cross-sectional.

Chapter 12 is effectively a random gathering of collected thoughts, offered to me in response to my 2009 survey. They are included with the full knowledge and permission of the contributors, for which the author is profoundly grateful.

These perceptions range from the personal ('I used to be very reluctant to kneel at the front') to the philosophical ('I see the mercy seat as a disappearing metaphor in our ministry').

Despite the lack of statistical viability, the author suggests that together these 13 contemporary reflections illustrate a number of important points for 21st-century Salvationists, including:

• Salvationists care about the mercy seat because it is important to them

   • there is no single definitive purpose for using the mercy seat

   • God is still willing to meet and transform people at the mercy seat.

Head Space

   1. What do the personal accounts tell you about mercy-seat use?

2. Which, if any, account connects with your own experience of the mercy seat?

3. Identify a section or phrase that you find particularly moving.

4. What issues or questions do these accounts raise about mercy-seat use in your corps?

Heart Space

Thank God that he values and honours the Army mercy seat.

Listen to God, to hear if he is asking you to look at mercy-seat use in a different way.

Ask God to make you increasingly sensitive and available to those who want to know more about him.

Chapter 13

Around a Common Mercy Seat – the Mercy Seat and Other Denominations

THE Army is not alone in benefiting from Brengle's holiness teaching. Nor are we alone in appreciating the value of mercy-seat response. For while the widespread use of the mourner's bench has long since dropped out of Methodist practice, a number of other denominations recognise the benefits not only of calling people in response to the preached word but also of providing a place for that response.

One of the main proponents of the mercy seat is the Church of the Nazarene, which calls the prayer bench at the front of its churches 'the altar'.

The altar is the architectural focal point of a Nazarene church in the way the mercy seat is up-front and central in the typical Salvation Army hall.

Nazarenes, like Salvationists, can trace their altar to the American revival of the early 1800s.

A Nazarene altar is used in the same way and for the same purposes as the mercy seat.

Unlike traditional Army mercy seats, Nazarene altars do not have inscriptions.

Head Space

1. The mercy seat is regarded as a distinctive of Salvation Army worship. As the Church of the Nazarene shows, the Army does not have the monopoly on mercy-seat use. What other aspects of Salvationist witness and worship exist in other denominations?

2. What aspects of Salvation Army worship and witness do you find particularly attractive and meaningful?

3. What, if anything, is unique about Salvation Army worship?

4. What aspects of worship and witness has the Army helpfully adopted and adapted from other parts of the universal Church?

Heart Space

Thank God for the work and witness of other denominations.

Thank God for the openness to, and sharing of, ways of winning people for Christ.

Pray for the worldwide mission of Christians everywhere to preach the gospel and make disciples.

Chapter 14

Pitfalls of Free Fall

SALVATIONISTS believe that people can respond to God at any time, at any place and in many different ways. They do not believe that response is determined or limited to right time, right place or right way.

While typically people use the mercy seat in response to an invitation given after a sermon, sometimes people go forward uninvited at an earlier point of a meeting. When this happens the meeting planned for the whole is often rescheduled for the sake of the one at the mercy seat.

Chapter 14 looks at some of the tensions of having such a free-fall approach to the mercy seat, and notes problems – many of them attitudinal – connected with mercy-seat use.

One danger is to attribute to the mercy seat a power it does not possess. The simple touching of the mercy seat (as some people might touch a statue, relic or icon) does not constitute a significant spiritual transaction.

The act of using the mercy seat does not intrinsically change the spiritual status of the seeker. People are not more holy for kneeling at a mercy seat. People do not have to go to the mercy seat to be saved.

The act of using the mercy seat should never be seen as an empty gesture, ritual or superstition.

The act of using the mercy seat should not be seen as an alternative to deeper obedience – such as mending a broken relationship in person.

The act of using the mercy seat should not be regarded as an alternative to taking personal responsibility.

Weak, take-it-or-leave-it invitations are not conducive to encouraging mercy-seat use.

One of the important correctives to mercy-seat misuse is to have a suitable, trained and sensitive counselling team.

Orders and Regulations for Local Officers states that 'all Salvationists should be qualified and trained to counsel seekers at the mercy seat at any time'.

Head Space

1. How helpful is a free-fall approach (people can use the mercy seat at any point in a meeting)? Would it be better if people were invited only after a sermon? Does the planned content of a meeting have to be adjusted because someone is using the mercy seat?

2. To what extent does attitude determine how often a mercy seat is used?

3. To what extent might using the mercy seat as a general place of prayer mask the fact that it is less used as a place for salvation?

4. What pressures are there on preachers not to invite people to the mercy seat?

5. What pressures are there on congregations to respond, and not to respond, at the mercy seat?

6. How could mercy-seat counselling be improved?

Heart Space

Pray for those who regularly prepare and preach the word of God at your corps.

Pray for those who counsel those who use the mercy seat.

Ask God to help you check, and where necessary challenge, your attitude towards those who use the mercy seat.

Chapter 15

The Mercy Seat and Creative Response 1

MEETING leaders are increasingly inviting Salvation Army congregations to respond to God in ways other than kneeling at the mercy seat.

Activities such as lighting a candle, writing a prayer, hammering a nail into a cross, washing one's hands or receiving a bookmark have become associated with what is called 'creative response'. Typically the responses involve members of the congregation leaving their seats and moving towards the front of the hall, or to another part of the hall. Sometimes the mercy seat is involved; sometimes it is not. Often a creative response is designed to fit the specific theme of the meeting.

Salvationist worship – typically and traditionally – involves the use of symbols, of which the mercy seat is one.

Matt Clifton writes: 'To use the mercy seat only as a place of repentance has made many long-term Salvationists reluctant to use it. We have to find pastoral methods for reshaping its meaning in worship.'

Creative response is seen as do-able. There seems to be no inner conflict about whether a person should go forward to, say, collect a stone or light a candle in the way there often is when a person feels under conviction to go to the mercy seat.

Creative response is seen as non-judgmental. One of the main reasons people do not use the mercy seat is through fear they will be judged or criticised for doing so.

Creative response, in which typically the majority of the congregation participates, offers safety in numbers.

By encouraging people to move, creative response can make people less reluctant to use the mercy seat.

Head Space

1. Why has creative response become popular?

2. What does creative response offer that the mercy seat does not?

3. How content would you be for creative response to replace mercy-seat use completely?

4. To what extent is creative response a fresh way of appealing to people's love of the symbolic?

5. To what extent do you understand what is being asked of you, and why, in a mercy-seat appeal and in an invitation to take part in a creative response?

Heart Space

Rejoice that God speaks to us in many ways and accepts the worship of our sincere hearts however we express it.

Thank God for the gift of creativity.

Offer your creativity, gifts, talent, time and energy to him afresh.

Chapter 16

The Mercy Seat and Creative Response 2

FOR many people the non-judgmental attitude that accompanies creative response is an incentive to respond to God physically within Salvationist worship. Creative response avoids embarrassment. It offers a sense of corporate worship and, through seeing people respond to God, a sense of worth for the meeting leader.

Each of these advantages raises issues.

Creative response is do-able but is there the same sense of Holy Spirit conviction that often precedes mercy-seat use?

Creative response does not require records of responders to be kept. This does not facilitate pastoral follow-up the way mercy-seat use does.

Creative response lacks the judgmentalism sometimes directed at – or perceived by – mercy-seat users. But how comfortable are those for whom creative response, especially if it involves the majority of the congregation, does not connect?

In 1996 the International Spiritual Life Commission discussed the observance of Holy Communion and baptism. Shaw Clifton argued that, if the Army were to reintroduce the sacraments, careful advance consideration would need to be given to a number of practical and theological questions. 'For any ritual we embrace or devise, what theology shall we attach to it?' he asks. 'What will we tell the Salvationists of the world is the spiritual meaning and significance of it? What will we tell them is happening in the ritual that did not happen and was not available to us before we embraced the ritual?'

While Salvationists are more likely to regard mercy-seat use as a spiritual exercise than a ritual, the general point still applies: whatever

Salvationists do in worship – including mercy-seat use and creative response – must have 'spiritual meaning and significance'.

Asking people to move to the front, or any other part, of the hall in response to God must mean something; otherwise it is an empty gesture – a meaningless ritual – the antithesis of Salvationist worship. Is it enough to be able to say that 'everybody went forward this morning', if nobody knows exactly what the 'going forward' means?

Head Space

1. What is the purpose of non-mercy-seat responses?

2. To what extent is a creative response an act of spiritual commitment?

3. What does a creative response offer that a mercy-seat response does not?

4. How, as the majority of the congregation respond by picking up a bookmark from the mercy seat or holiness table, or any other typical creative response, can someone indicate that they want to find faith in Christ?

5. To what extent is creative response an easy answer to lack of mercy-seat use?

6. To what extent is creative response likely to replace the mercy seat as the focus of Salvationist response?

Heart Space

Rejoice that God speaks to us in many ways and accepts the worship of our sincere hearts however we express it.

Thank God for the gift of creativity.

Offer your creativity, gifts, talent, time and energy to him afresh.

Chapter 17

Refreshed and Fed?

TODAY'S Salvationists use the mercy seat for reasons other than salvation and sanctification. The burning question for some today is whether the mercy seat, generally regarded as a place of grace, has become a means of grace – a sacrament – in the minds of those who use it. Put simply, is the mercy seat the Salvationist's sacrament?

The Salvation Army's view is that all of life is a sacrament and that it is the inner experience which ecclesiastical sacraments represent that is essential to salvation and sanctification.

Most Protestant denominations observe two sacraments: baptism and Holy Communion. The Catholic Church (Roman and Anglo) observes seven: baptism, confirmation, Holy Communion, reconciliation (formerly known as 'confession'), marriage, holy orders and anointing the sick (formerly known as 'extreme unction'). They are regarded as the means – the channels – by which God delivers his grace to a believer.

There are, however, occasions when mercy-seat use connects with some of the truths these sacraments represent.

Baptism: is a mark that a new life as a follower of Christ has begun. While Evangeline Booth likened the mercy seat to a baptismal font, Salvationists do not believe that the act of kneeling at a mercy seat makes someone a Christian; nor that a person has to kneel at a mercy seat to be saved.

Confirmation: is the occasion when a person confirms the promises made on their behalf when they were baptised. The mercy seat is a place where people make and renew promises to God. It is also the place where God confirms – or empowers – people with the indwelling power of his Holy Spirit.

Holy Communion: is a commemoration of the atoning death of Jesus. Evangeline Booth wrote: 'The penitent form is our Communion rail, where the broken links of fellowship are united: where grudge-bearing has been lost, the enemy forgiven, the estranged ones reconciled.' The mercy seat is the place where people can and do get saved.

Holy orders: is the ordaining of people to specific roles and ministries within the Church. While Salvationists believe in the priesthood of all believers, the mercy seat is often used as a place of personal covenant with God in respect of lifestyle and service. Salvationists often kneel at the mercy seat to sign Junior Soldier promise cards, Soldier's Covenants and Officer's Covenants.

Marriage: although married Salvationists might not see themselves as 'ministers of a sacrament' to their spouses as Catholic couples do, some make praying together at the mercy seat their first united act as a married couple within a wedding ceremony.

Anointing the sick: although anointing those who are sick by using oil at an Army mercy seat is not a common practice, the mercy seat is a place where people make special prayers for healing, either for themselves or for others.

Reconciliation: while Salvationists believe that absolution from sin is the prerogative of God and not of an intermediary, they also acknowledge the benefit of publicly kneeling at the mercy seat to confess their sins privately to God and receiving from him the assurance of his forgiveness.

Head Space

1. Thinking of the occasions that you have used the mercy seat, which of the above sacraments best describe the reasons for your visit?

2. What other uses does the mercy seat have beyond the seven sacraments listed above?

3. Which, if any, of the seven sacraments do you think does not apply to mercy-seat use, and why?

4. How useful, when applied to mercy-seat use, is the advice given to Richard Burridge regarding Anglican communicants: 'All may, none must, some should'?

Heart Space

Thank God for the rich diversity of response to him through different church traditions.

Pray that all aspects of your service – the things you do for God – do not become ends in themselves but are and remain outward expressions of your inner faith.

Chapter 18

A Place of Grace or a Means of Grace?

IN Chapter 17 we looked at a connection between mercy-seat use and ecclesiastical sacraments. This chapter considers further discussion about whether or not mercy-seat use is a sacrament.

The *Oxford English Dictionary* defines 'sacrament' as 'a religious ceremony or act of the Christian Churches regarded as an outward and visible sign of inward and spiritual grace'.

Augustine of Hippo (354-430) said: 'In no religion, whether true or false, can people be held together in association, unless they are gathered together with some common share in some visible signs or sacraments.' One of those 'visible signs' that provides Salvationists around the world with a shared identity is the mercy seat – it is to be found in every territory in which the Army is at work.

'The Call to the Mercy Seat', issued by the International Spiritual Life Commission of 1998, reads: 'We call Salvationists worldwide to recognise the wide understanding of the mercy seat that God has given to the Army; to rejoice that Christ uses this means of grace to confirm his presence; and to ensure that its spiritual benefits are fully explored in every corps and Army centre.'

Lutheran and Reformed theology understands 'means of grace' as being the preaching of the word of God and the sacraments of baptism and the Lord's Supper. The Roman Catholic view of 'means of grace' is that the observance of the sacraments are the means by which a person can be saved and subsequently sustained in their faith.

John Wesley (*The Works of Wesley, Vol 5, Sermon 16*) defines 'means of grace' as 'prayer, searching the Scriptures, receiving the

Lord's Supper – eating bread and drinking wine in remembrance of Him'.

Some Salvationists see a close connection between mercy-seat use and the sacraments of baptism and/or Holy Communion.

Ecclesiastical sacramental worship, however, depends on things being right – right time, right place, right person (giving and receiving) and right words. In contrast, the mercy seat is available to everyone at any part of a meeting – and even before its commencement or after its conclusion.

At the heart of worship is not what we do – whether that is to partake of sacraments, make music or use the mercy seat – but who we are. Any worship or spiritual activity can become a show, an empty gesture or meaningless ritual. The challenge is in not allowing it to be.

Head Space

1. To what extent is mercy-seat use a 'means of grace'?

2. To what extent, if any, has the mercy seat as a 'place of grace' become a means of grace?

3. What 'visible signs' do Salvationists share and what do they signify?

4. In this chapter, contributors liken the mercy seat to a rosary, an altar, a baptismal font, a baptistry for believer's baptism, a Communion rail, an ammunition factory, a focal point. Which, if any, of these do you find accurate and helpful?

5. To what extent does it matter if people regard the mercy seat as a sacrament?

6. To what extent is following Jesus based on doing rather than being?

Heart Space

Thank God for the gift of senses – sight, hearing, touch, smell, taste – the means by which we connect with the world.

Thank God for his willingness to connect with us through our senses and by his Spirit with our spirit.

38

Ask God to challenge you about the way you express your faith.

Ask God to renew your love for him and discover/rediscover the joy of being his child.

Chapter 19

The Mercy Seat in The Old Testament

AS Chapter 19 forms the basis of a Bible study, it is not the intention here to have a study guide to a study guide!

For many Christians the Old Testament is like an iceberg – they know where the obvious parts are, usually based on the life stories of characters such as Moses, Abraham and David – but there's an awful lot that is unfathomed, especially regarding how and where events fit historically and theologically.

It is beyond the scope of this chapter to offer a comprehensive guide to the Old Testament. However, the Ark of the Covenant (with its mercy seat) is just one of the ways God speaks about atonement and salvation in advance of the arrival of Jesus.

Luke's Gospel solves another mystery: What did Jesus do in the forty days between his resurrection and his ascension? Answer: He taught his disciples how he fulfilled everything that is written about him in the three parts of the Old Testament – the law, prophets and psalms (24:44-47).

Throughout the Old Testament there are hints, models, parallels, prototypes and shadows of the salvation Jesus would ultimately bring. Estimates of how many Old Testament prophecies were fulfilled in Jesus range from around 40 to 300.

The author calculates that each of the 39 books of the Old Testament contains the message of salvation or points in some way to Jesus. The use of the mercy seat on the Day of Atonement (Leviticus 16) is one such indication. Some of the others are outlined here as signposts and incentives to further insight.

41

Genesis 3:15 Adam and Eve

After the Fall, God tells the serpent that he will send someone to 'crush your head'.

Widely reckoned to be the first prophecy regarding the coming of Jesus, this statement shows God's intent to restore the fellowship that existed before the Fall and to destroy for ever the source – and remove the consequences – of sin.

Genesis 6 The Flood

God responds to universal wickedness (v5), corruption and violence (v11) by grieving over his creation and flooding the Earth. A righteous and blameless man, Noah – along with his family – is spared. He builds an ark, fills it with his family and animals and survives the destruction. After the floodwaters subside, the Earth is repopulated. God enters a new covenant – of which the rainbow is the sign – never to destroy the Earth by flood again (9:11-13).

The banishment of Adam and Eve and the Flood are early indications of God's attitude to sin. By virtue of the fact that Adam, Eve, Noah and his family were not wiped out, these accounts also suggest a divine propensity towards forgiveness. Noah exercising faith – he built an ark in a desert with no rain in sight – is an element in his salvation. Jesus recognises the attitudes of those times in this reference to his Second Coming: 'Just as it was in the days of Noah, so also will it be in the days of the Son of Man' (Luke 17:26).

Genesis 22 Abraham and Isaac

In obedience to God, Abraham takes his only son up Mount Moriah to offer him as a sacrifice. With Isaac on the altar, God tells Abraham to take a ram and offer it in Isaac's place. Abraham sacrifices the ram. Isaac lives.

While not the first time an animal is offered in sacrifice (Abel offers a lamb in Genesis 4:4) the elements of an only son, a mountain, a sheep which dies in the place of a person and a God who accepts that sacrifice suggest a close parallel with and a foreshadowing of Calvary.

Exodus 12:1-13 The Passover

God promises the Children of Israel that he will deliver them from the harshness and death of slavery. On the evening this is to happen, each family is to kill a spotless male lamb and smear its blood on the doorframe of the family home. That night they are to stay in their houses, ready to leave. God will pass through Egypt and strike down every firstborn. Everyone who shelters under the blood will be saved.

God-appointed sacrifice (the killing of a spotless lamb) and the exercise of personal faith (sheltering under its blood) are the foundations upon which the Children of Israel are subsequently able to cross the Red Sea, escape slavery and head towards the Promised Land.

In the New Testament, Jesus – the 'Lamb of God, who takes away the sin of the world' (John 1:29) – is God's appointed paschal sacrifice. Those who, by act of personal faith, trust in his redemptive death and resurrection are saved – 'The blood of Jesus, his Son, purifies us from all sin' (1 John 1:7).

Numbers 21 The Bronze Snake

The journey to the Promised Land was not going well. Many of the Children of Israel were impatient with God and Moses. God 'sent venomous snakes among them' (v6). The people recognise their sin and ask for a solution. God tells Moses to make a replica serpent and put it on a pole. If anyone who has been bitten looks up at the bronze snake they will live.

The elements of sin, consequent death, repentance, a God-appointed solution, a lifting up, a personal choice and exercise of faith by the one who is going to die to look away or to look up and live are suggestions of a greater lifting-up. Jesus certainly thought so. In John 3:15 he says: 'As Moses lifted up the snake in the desert, so the Son of Man must be lifted up, that everyone who believes in him may have eternal life.'

To this we can also add the cities of refuge of Joshua 20, the story of Jonah, the pierced hands and feet of Psalm 22, the 'son of man' in Daniel 7 and the Man of Sorrows of Isaiah 53 – and still only scratch the surface.

Far from being separate and isolated accounts of the divine intention towards humankind, the Old and New Testaments are inexorably and intricately connected.

Heart Space

Thank God for the gift of life.

Thank God for the loving-kindness that longs for people to choose to live with him.

Thank God for the grace that reaches out to you, offering you the assurance of sins forgiven, power to live for him and the promise of life with him.

Ask God to show you how best to live in response to him.

Chapter 20

The Mercy Seat in The New Testament

AS previously stated, it is not the intention here to replicate the Bible study content contained in the respective chapter of *The Mercy Seat Revisited*.

In the Old Testament the mercy seat is the place of blood-bought reconciliation and its Hebrew word *kapporeth*, (from *kaphar*) meaning 'cover', is the Old Testament word for 'atonement'. *Kaphar* is one of the three Old Testament words for 'forgive'. The others are *nasa* ('to lift away') and *salach* ('to carry away'). So, in the Old Testament, God deals with sin by covering it, lifting it away or carrying it away.

Let's consider some of the New Testament word-pictures of forgiveness.

Covering

Forgiveness is a covering or hiding of sin. It says in 1 Peter 4:8: 'Love covers over a multitude of sins.' In Romans 4:7, Paul quotes Psalm 32: 'Blessed are they whose transgressions are forgiven, whose sins are covered.' James says: 'Whoever turns a sinner from the error of his way will save him from death and cover over a multitude of sins' (5:20).

God covering our sins is not a cover-up. It is a thorough dealing with them – a hiding away; out of sight and out of mind.

Atoning

In many translations, the Greek word *hilasterion* of Hebrews 9:5 appears as 'mercy seat'. This rendering first appeared in the 1535 *Coverdale Bible* as 'Mercyseate'. Subsequent versions, including the *Geneva Bible* (1560), the *Bishops' Bible* (1568), the *King James Bible*

(1611), the *Revised Standard Version* (1952) and the *Living Bible* (1971), also use the same term.

The only other occasion the word is used in the New Testament is in Romans 3:25 where Paul, referring to Jesus, writes: 'God presented him as a sacrifice of atonement, through faith in his blood.' The *King James Bible* renders it: 'Whom God hath set forth to be a propitiation, through faith in his blood.'

To propitiate is to appease an offended person. God accepts the sacrifice of Jesus as the means by which he is appeased. Jesus' death is the God-ordained and God-accepted prerequisite that allows for sinful humans to be at one with the sinless divine.

Clearing Debt

The most common New Testament word for forgiveness is *aphesis*. Literally meaning 'send from', it is also used for the clearing of a debt. In Matthew 6:12, Jesus teaches his disciples to ask God to 'forgive us our debts, as we also have forgiven our debtors'. Jesus uses the same metaphor in his parable of the unmerciful servant (Matthew 18:21-35).

Every time we sin, our account with God goes further into debit. When he forgives us, he does more than cancel the debt; he puts us in credit – we become inheritors of treasure in Heaven.

Taking Away

In Leviticus 16, the sins of the people are figuratively laid upon the scapegoat. It is sent away into the wilderness to die. Referring to the events on the Day of Atonement, the writer to the Hebrews says: 'It is impossible for the blood of bulls and goats to take away sins' (Hebrews 10:4). In John 1:29, John the Baptist refers to Jesus as 'the Lamb of God, who takes away the sin of the world'.

When we are forgiven God takes away the weight of sin – lifts the burden of guilt – from us.

Setting Free

In Romans 6:18-23 and 7:14, Paul describes people as being slaves to sin. The wages paid to sin-slaves is death (6:23). The book of Revelation, by contrast, opens with the declaration that Jesus has 'freed us from our sins by his blood' (1:5). Sin has the power to enslave a person. Sin fuels addictions and hurtful habits; it shapes thought processes, which is why Paul urges believers to 'take every thought captive' (2 Corinthians 10:5) and to be transformed from the world's standards by the renewal of their minds (Romans 12:2).

Sin captures a person, holds them in captivity and enslaves them. By his death and resurrection, Jesus has broken the power of sin and death. He redeems us. When we are forgiven, we are set free.

Washing

The songwriter asks: 'What can wash away my sin?' He concludes: 'Nothing but the blood of Jesus.' In Acts 22:16, after Paul's conversion, Ananias tells him to 'be baptised and wash your sins away, calling on his name'. It is the calling on the name of Jesus that brings forgiveness, rather than the act of baptism – as Paul himself quotes from Joel in Romans 10:13 ('Everyone who calls on the name of the Lord will be saved'). John writes that the 'blood of Jesus... purifies us from all sin' (1 John 1:7). In Hebrews 1:3 Jesus sits at God's right hand 'after he had provided purification for sins'.

Although New Testament baptism and Old Testament purification rituals signify different things, the basic idea is that sin stains and pollutes – it makes us feel dirty – but that when we are forgiven we are cleansed and clean.

Delivering

The idea of being delivered or rescued is central to the concept of being saved. Just as the disciples wanted Jesus to save them from drowning (Matthew 8:25), so the same word *sozo* – and its associate *soteria* (salvation) – is used to describe spiritual deliverance from death. Mary's child is to be called Jesus 'because he will save his people from their sins' (Matthew 1:21). The angels announce 'a Saviour has been born to you; he is Christ the Lord' (Luke 2:11). Regarding Jesus, Paul announces, 'Salvation [*soteria*] is found in no one else, for there is no other name under heaven given to men by which we must be saved [*sozo*]' (Acts 4:12).

To be forgiven is to be rescued from the consequences of sin – death.

Grace

The last New Testament word-picture to consider is also the underlying principle for all biblical images of forgiveness. Without this word this study would not only be lacking but also potentially misleading.

Its only Gospel appearance is in Luke 7:43. In the *New International Version*, it is lost in translation: 'I suppose the one who had the bigger debt cancelled.' In the *King James Bible* it is rendered: 'I suppose that he, to whom he forgave most', where the word for 'forgave' is *charizomai*. The word means to bestow a favour unconditionally. Its linguistic cousin is *charis* – 'grace'.

Whatever the biblical picture, the principle is the same. It is only because of God's grace – his unconditional favour – that we can be saved.

Maybe this spiritual truth influenced Bible translator William Tyndale, when in his 1526 New Testament he rendered the *hilasterion* of Hebrews 9:5 as 'seat of grace'.

Paul spells this out in Ephesians: 'For it is by grace [*charis*] you have been saved [*sozo*], through faith – and this not from yourselves, it is the gift of God – not by works, so that no one can boast' (2:8-9).

There is nothing we can do to earn our way into Heaven. There is no ceremony we can submit to, no heritage to depend on and no religious service to offer that will make God forgive us or subvert the need for his forgiveness. There is no sin too small that we can ignore. There is no sin too big that he can't forgive.

The underlying message of the gospel – foreshadowed in the Old Testament, fulfilled in the New – is that for no reason other than his grace, God has provided the means of our forgiveness in the form of his sinless Son, has accepted his obedient death and offers hell-bound sinners the choice of eternal life.

Forgiveness is a free gift from God. It is available to all who turn from their wrongdoing, ask his forgiveness and put their trust in him.

Heart Space

Thank God for his grace – his willingness to be at one with us.
Confess your sins to him and ask for his forgiveness.

Ask God to empower you with his Holy Spirit to withstand temptation.

Agree with God that with his help you will continue to follow him and make his lifestyle yours.

Pray for those you know who need to find salvation.

Chapter 21

Next?

IN this study guide we have covered many aspects of Salvationist worship and ministry – corporate and personal. We have looked at some of the basic scriptural foundations that underpin the purpose and practice of The Salvation Army.

We have looked at some spiritual principles of Salvationist worship. We have traced humankind's sense of wanting to reach out and respond to its Creator from the earliest pages of the Bible to the erection of roadside shrines for 21st-century accident victims. We have seen that as society and culture change, so the Army has moved with it.

Salvationists appreciate the value of special, spiritual journeys. Salvationists, on the whole, value the availability of the mercy seat and the significant journeys that are made to the mercy seat.

Salvationists believe that while mercy-seat use is helpful it is not essential to salvaation nor a necessary step towards being saved. We believe in an any-time-any-place-any-how God. We don't always know how best to put those two ideas together.

The Salvation Army belongs to the preach-for-a-verdict school of preaching. Historically, sermons have included an invitation to respond to God there and then and the mercy seat has been the destination of such response.

Salvationists need to work out the relationship between mercy-seat use and creative response.

If the mercy seat is to be used more, some practical measures may need to be enacted to allow for this.

Just as the Army's past has been shaped by how and how often the mercy seat has been used, so will its future.

Head Space

1. To what extent has your attitude to the place of the mercy seat in Salvationist worship changed over the course of this study?

2. To what extent has your attitude towards those who use the mercy seat changed over the course of this study?

3. How do you see mercy-seat use in the future?

4. To what extent are you more likely to use the mercy seat in the future?

5. What measures could your corps consider to make the mercy seat more accessible, and mercy-seat use more frequent and more meaningful?

6. Would you be happy for people to sit and pray on your corps mercy seat? If not, why not?

Heart Space

Thank God for the new insights you have discovered by reading this book.

Agree with God that what you have discovered will be more than head knowledge, but something you will put into practice.

Thank God for his willingness to accept all of our sincere responses to him.

Ask God for wisdom and insight as to how best to share the gospel in your community.

Ask God for the grace and power of the Holy Spirit to enable that to happen.

Pray for those you know who need to find salvation.